Ludwig van Beethoven

YOUNG COMPOSER

Ludwig van Beethoven

YOUNG COMPOSER

by Louis Sabin
illustrated by Ellen Beier

Troll Associates

Library of Congress Cataloging-in-Publication Data

Sabin, Louis.
    Ludwig van Beethoven—young composer / by Louis Sabin;
illustrated by Ellen Beier.
      p.   cm.
    Summary: Traces the life and musical career of the celebrated
nineteenth-century German composer.
    ISBN 0-8167-2511-X (lib. bdg.)   ISBN 0-8167-2512-8 (pbk.)
    1. Beethoven, Ludwig van, 1770-1827—Juvenile literature.
2. Composers—Austria—Biography—Juvenile literature.
[1. Beethoven, Ludwig van, 1770-1827. 2. Composers.] I. Beier,
Ellen, ill. II. Title.
ML3930.B4S18 1992
780′.92—dc20
[B]   91-18616

Ludwig van Beethoven

YOUNG COMPOSER

The music soared. The sound of the huge orchestra and chorus filled the theater. Four solo singers—the finest in all of Europe—sang the most glorious music ever written for the human voice. It was the music of Ludwig van Beethoven, the leading composer of the nineteenth century. And the great genius himself was conducting the performance.

The audience that filled Vienna's Kärnthnerthor
Theater was thrilled by the music. This was the
first performance of Beethoven's Ninth Symphony.
On that spring evening of May 7, 1824, musical
history was being made. The audience was proud
to be part of it. And when the closing notes echoed
through the theater, the people stood and gave the
composer a rousing ovation. Wave after wave of
applause surged toward the stage.

Through it all, Beethoven stood motionless, facing the orchestra. At last, one of the solo singers realized what was happening. She walked over to Beethoven and gently placed a hand on his shoulder. Then she turned Beethoven to face the audience, which continued to applaud and shout his name. Only then did Beethoven smile and bow. Only then did he know his symphony was a huge success.

Beethoven could not hear the applause of the adoring audience. He could not hear the orchestra that lovingly played his inspiring music, or the singers who sang his notes. The great composer was totally deaf. The most brilliant, beautiful music ever written came from a man who had lost his hearing many years before. To his thousands of admirers, it seemed like a miracle.

Music was always the center of Ludwig van Beethoven's life. His father, Johann, was a singer and music teacher. His grandfather, Ludwig, for whom the boy was named, was a singer and orchestra conductor. Music was the family business. No subject interested the Beethovens more than music. So it was no surprise that little Ludwig was trained to be a musician from his earliest childhood.

Ludwig van Beethoven was born on December 16, 1770, in the city of Bonn, Germany. His mother was happy that Ludwig was a healthy baby. She had given birth to two other children before him. But both died soon after birth. In those days it was not unusual for babies to live just a short time. Mrs. Beethoven had five more children after Ludwig. Only two of them lived to be adults. They were Caspar Carl, who was born in 1774, and Nickolaus Johann, who was born two years later.

Mrs. Beethoven led a sad life. She thought about the children who did not survive. She worried about the health of her three boys. And she had a hard time feeding and caring for the family. There was never enough money.

Mr. Beethoven's income was very small. It barely covered their basic expenses. Some months the Beethovens could not pay all their bills. It was not only that Ludwig's father was paid poorly. He also spent too much of his money on the wrong things. Johann van Beethoven was an alcoholic. This made things hard for the whole family.

Young Ludwig did not know why his mother was always unhappy. The little boy adored his gentle and caring mother, and he wanted to bring happiness into her life. He tried to be as good as possible, and not to bother or upset her.

15

Ludwig was also close to his grandfather. Old Ludwig van Beethoven was not a patient man, except with his little grandson. He loved the child and enjoyed playing with him. Grandfather Ludwig and his namesake were often seen walking around Bonn.

This was not the way Grandfather Beethoven treated his own son. Ludwig and Johann did not get along at all. Johann was a great disappointment to old Ludwig, who was a talented and successful musician. Ludwig was the choirmaster and orchestra leader at the court of the Elector of Cologne. The elector ruled one of the many small kingdoms that made up Germany in the eighteenth century.

Old Ludwig van Beethoven wanted his son Johann to be a fine court musician, like himself. This job paid a good salary. But Johann was not good enough to succeed his father. He was just an average singer, and he was not a very good music teacher. Even though it wasn't fair to punish Johann for this, his father never forgave him for not being great.

From the day baby Ludwig was born, everyone in the family watched him for signs of musical talent. They wanted him to be another Mozart. Wolfgang Amadeus Mozart began playing the piano when he was just five years old. He earned a lot of money as a child musician. Many families tried to turn their children into little Mozarts. To do that, they taught their children to play musical instruments while they were still toddlers.

Ludwig's musical training began when he was four years old. The Beethovens lived in the upstairs apartment of a two-family house on Rheingasse (German for Rhine Street). The Fischer family, who owned the house, lived downstairs. The Fischers' daughter, Cäcilia, was about the same age as Ludwig. When she was an adult, she spoke of the little boy who lived upstairs.

Cäcilia remembered when Ludwig started taking music lessons. She described "a tiny boy, standing on a little footstool in front of the clavier, to which his father had condemned him." (The clavier is a keyboard instrument like the modern piano.) Others who knew the Beethovens told the same story. Mr. Beethoven was a hard taskmaster. He insisted that the child spend hours every day practicing his music.

Ludwig both hated and loved his music lessons. Sometimes he got so tired of standing and playing that he began to cry. But there were times when he did not want to stop playing, even though he was tired. He really enjoyed the sounds he made on the clavier.

The next year, when he was five, Ludwig began
daily lessons on the violin. His father was also his
violin teacher. Now even more of the little boy's
day was devoted to studying music. He spent at
least one hour at the clavier. Then he practiced
the violin for another hour or more.

Ludwig also had to learn how to read music and how to transpose, or change, musical notes from one key to another. Johann Beethoven wanted his son to be able to play any music the first time he saw it. This meant that the boy had to have a full understanding of the language and theory of music.

When Mozart was a child, he was able to play any music put in front of him. He could play it in a high key or a low key. He could turn a march into a dance tune. He was also able to look at music written for any instrument and play it on the clavier.

Johann Beethoven wanted Ludwig to be as brilliant as Mozart. In fact, he wanted Ludwig to be even better than the marvelous Mozart. Young Mozart was a genius on one instrument. Young Ludwig was being trained to be a genius on two instruments.

Ludwig did show signs of musical genius. Almost as soon as he started learning to play the clavier, he began to compose his own music. But his father did not understand this kind of genius. This made Ludwig sad. When Beethoven was a grown man, he told a friend, "My beloved grandfather died when I was very young. He was so wise in music. He was so good to me. If he had lived, he would have lifted my spirits. Alas, nobody understood that my young head had more music in it than my little fingers could play."

Once, young Ludwig was trying to play new chords on the clavier. This made his father angry. "More of your fooling around?" Mr. Beethoven yelled. "Go away or I'll box your ears!"

Another time, Ludwig was playing one of his own tunes on the violin. His father rushed into the room and told the boy to stop. "What silly trash are you scraping at now? You know I can't bear that. Scrape according to the notes, otherwise your scraping won't amount to much."

Each time he was scolded, Ludwig stopped his musical experiments for a while. The boy really wanted to please his father. Maybe, he thought, writing tunes *was* a waste of time. Ludwig was far too young to know if his music was good or bad. He only knew that he heard melodies and harmonies in his head, and he wanted others to hear them.

Music mattered more than anything else to Ludwig. He continued to practice. He also continued to compose his own violin music. At the same time, his father tried to be more patient with the boy. Mr. Beethoven really wanted to be a good, loving father. So when he heard Ludwig playing a strange melody on the violin instead of practicing his scales, Mr. Beethoven spoke in a quiet voice. "Can you not stop, after all I've told you?" he asked.

Instead of answering, Ludwig played the tune again and smiled at his father. This tune, he was sure, his father would like.

But his father sighed. "That is something you made up yourself, isn't it?" he said. "You are not to do that yet. Apply yourself to the clavier and violin. Strike the notes quickly and correctly; that is more important. When you have once got so far, then you can and must work with your head."

His father gently placed a hand on young Ludwig's arm. "Don't concern yourself with your own music now," he said. "You are not to do that yet."

After that, Ludwig tried even harder to please his father. He practiced his lessons with great care. And when he heard his own music in his head, he simply sang it to himself. Someday, he thought, others will hear my music. Then Papa will be proud of me.

Ludwig did not spend all day with his music. He also went to a school called a Latin school. There he learned reading, writing, arithmetic, French, and Latin. In eighteenth century Germany, very few students went further than elementary school. Ludwig's formal schooling stopped when he was eleven years old.

Nobody knows how Ludwig felt about his schooling. We do know he was not an outstanding pupil. He was a poor speller all his life. His handwriting was not very good, and he did not seem to know much arithmetic.

Ludwig did remember much of the French and Latin he learned, as well as the poetry he read in school. The languages and poetry proved useful in later years. Latin was the language of the church. The adult Beethoven composed church music to be sung in Latin. And he set a number of poems to music. These are still sung in concert halls all over the world.

Ludwig was a quiet, shy boy. He watched everything that went on around him. But he seldom joined in games or sports with classmates. He thought a great deal more than he spoke. He liked to daydream and was often off in a world of his own.

When Beethoven was a famous man, his classmates were proud to say they knew him and had
gone to school with him. Still, not one of them
remembered young Ludwig ever playing, skating,
fishing, or even taking part in things like
snowball fights.

But there were some people who knew a different Ludwig. One was Cäcilia Fischer's brother, Gottfried. He remembered the Beethoven brothers as mischievous pranksters. Gottfried's mother kept chickens in the back yard. For a while she noticed that the hens did not seem to be laying as many eggs as usual. She kept watch and one day caught Ludwig in the yard.

"Ludwig, what are you up to there?" she asked.

Ludwig made up a very confusing story about his brother Caspar throwing Ludwig's handkerchief out a window and the handkerchief landing right near the hen house. He added that hens like to hide their eggs and that Mrs. Fischer would be happy when she found the hidden eggs. Then he said there were foxes in the neighborhood and foxes like to steal hens' eggs. So if she didn't find any eggs, the foxes must have taken them.

By the time Ludwig finished his long, silly excuse, Mrs. Fischer was giggling. "You are right about sly foxes," she said. "I think I am looking at one right now. And since you understand how foxes behave, I'm sure you will think of a way to stop them from stealing any more eggs." Then, still smiling, she went back into the house. Mrs. Fischer's kind words worked. No more eggs disappeared from the hen house.

Gottfried Fischer also remembered Ludwig playing games with his own brothers and the Fischer children. But mostly, Fischer said, Ludwig was alone, practicing his music. "One could not say that Ludwig cared much for companions or society," he said. "His happiest hours were those when he was free from the company of his parents —when all the family was away and he was alone by himself."

When Mr. Beethoven decided Ludwig was ready to play in public, the boy began giving concerts. The music part was fun for him. But the rest of it was hard work. Ludwig was not good with people. He did not smile much. He felt poor and badly dressed in front of the rich, important audiences. Most of all, Ludwig needed praise from his father. Instead, Mr. Beethoven only told him what he did wrong.

Sometimes Ludwig was the only performer. Other times, he shared the stage with another child who was studying music with Mr. Beethoven. Ludwig was a good musician, but it was soon clear that he needed a better teacher. Even Mr. Beethoven knew this was true. So at the age of eight Ludwig started to study piano and organ with other teachers.

One of Ludwig's new teachers was Mr. van den Eeden, the court organist for the Elector of Cologne. Mr. van den Eeden was calm and gentle with his young pupil. At each lesson Ludwig spent part of the time playing an instrument. But that wasn't all. Mr. van den Eeden encouraged the boy to do creative things with music.

The teacher first asked Ludwig to play a piece of music as it was written. Then he told the boy to take it home and study it well. At the next lesson, he was to play it in different styles. "Imagine that you are George Frederick Handel," said Mr. van den Eeden. "Write it in Handel's style. Then play it. Next, do the same thing as if you are Johann Sebastian Bach. Finally, my young maestro, let me hear how Ludwig van Beethoven writes and plays this music!"

Ludwig enjoyed the challenge and the chance to have fun with music. At last he was able to do what he did best—compose!

Ludwig looked forward to every lesson. He had many questions, and Mr. van den Eeden was delighted to answer them. Ludwig was just the kind of pupil a teacher hopes for.

At the age of ten, Ludwig began studying with other advanced teachers. For the first time in his young life, Ludwig was totally happy. He glowed under the praise of his teachers. He never tired of music.

One day Ludwig brought one of his teachers the sheet music of an organ work he had just written. It was so difficult that the teacher was puzzled. "Why, you can't play that, Ludwig," the teacher told him. The boy answered, "I will when I am bigger."

Most composers have to play their music to know how it sounds. Ludwig did not need to play the notes on an instrument to be able to hear them. He heard them clearly in his head. Even as a young boy, he was able to create a complete, complicated piece of work in his mind. This was the first sign of his genius as a composer.

When he was eleven years old, Ludwig began helping at church services. Any time the regular organists were not able to play, Ludwig took their place. He often accompanied the singing of the Mass, a little boy dwarfed by the immense organ. The only payment he received was permission to practice the organ when there were no services being held. He felt that this was payment enough.

One time, while accompanying the Mass, Ludwig stunned his listeners. A musician who was there described what he heard. "The boy took a theme and developed it, to the amazement of the church orchestra." Everyone was impressed. The boy was allowed to play on and on, adding new themes as he went along. "That," said the musician, "was the opening of his brilliant career."

In 1782, when Ludwig was twelve years old, he became assistant court organist. He was pleased at the honor of being chosen and by the salary he was paid. The next year, he was appointed as the accompanist to the Bonn Opera. His family welcomed the income. From then on, Ludwig was the main source of income for the Beethovens. He was glad to be able to make life easier for his mother and younger brothers.

In the next few years, Ludwig van Beethoven
became well known in the world of music. He
played the viola in the Bonn Theater orchestra.
He taught music to a number of children in the
city. He continued as court organist. And he kept
composing his own music.

Beethoven was a teenager when he first noticed
a problem with his hearing. For a while there
was a buzzing and humming in his ears. After a
while the annoying sounds disappeared. But they
returned later, and his hearing became worse
and worse.

Today, doctors believe that Beethoven's adult deafness was the result of a childhood ear infection. Many young children get ear infections when they have the flu or other common diseases. Now we treat these infections with antibiotics, and they do not cause serious problems later in life. But antibiotics did not exist in Beethoven's time.

Until 1802, when Beethoven was thirty-two years old, his hearing loss did not harm his career. He was a famous composer and musician. He gave many performances of his own music and that of other great composers. Each year, his work became more magnificent. His earliest compositions were in the same style as two musical giants, Haydn and Mozart. But as he matured, Beethoven's own musical voice came through more clearly. His genius produced works for the piano, the violin, and for large orchestras and small groups of musicians. He wrote songs for single voices or for huge choruses.

EAR TRUMPETS

Marvelous music poured out of Beethoven's soul. There was nothing in his life besides music— no family, no permanent home. Music was all that mattered. But each year his hearing grew dimmer. He tried using ear trumpets to magnify the sounds around him. He had a special hearing aid made, a carved piece of wood attached to the bottom of the piano. This made it possible for him to feel the vibrations produced by the piano as he played it. But these aids, like all the treatments doctors prescribed, did nothing to help.

As deafness descended like a thick fog around Beethoven, his days as a performer ended. But he still had his ability to compose. For the last ten years of his life, until he died on March 26, 1827, Beethoven added to the brilliant treasury of his music. Altogether, his works included nine symphonies, five piano concertos, one violin concerto, one opera, two Masses, thirty-five songs for solo voice, thirty-two piano sonatas, seventeen string quartets, and hundreds of other musical works.

Beethoven's musical voice rings clear and true. His music inspires, thrills, soothes, and delights listeners young and old. Ludwig van Beethoven's music will live forever...for the world to hear.